I AM Love
A Children's Guide of Positive Affirmations
Copyright © 2019 Jasmin Porter
All rights reserved. No part of this book may be used, reproduced, distributed, photocopied, recorded, or used by any other electronic or mechanical methods without the prior written permission of the publisher except in the case of brief quotations embodied in crtical articles or reviews. Each character in this book was created purely from the authors imagination and do not represent any living or deceased human being. The characters also do not represent any other fictional character that was not created by the author of this book.

For more information contact:
Jasmin Porter through email at: jasminflower11@yahoo.com
ISBN: 978-0-578-55620-8 (paperback)

This book is dedicated to

My mother, my father, my children and the children of the world. And to the children of the world who are seeds for our future, may you remain kind, humble, and live in peace. May you thrive with acts of kindness guided by Love.
For Love is the only way!

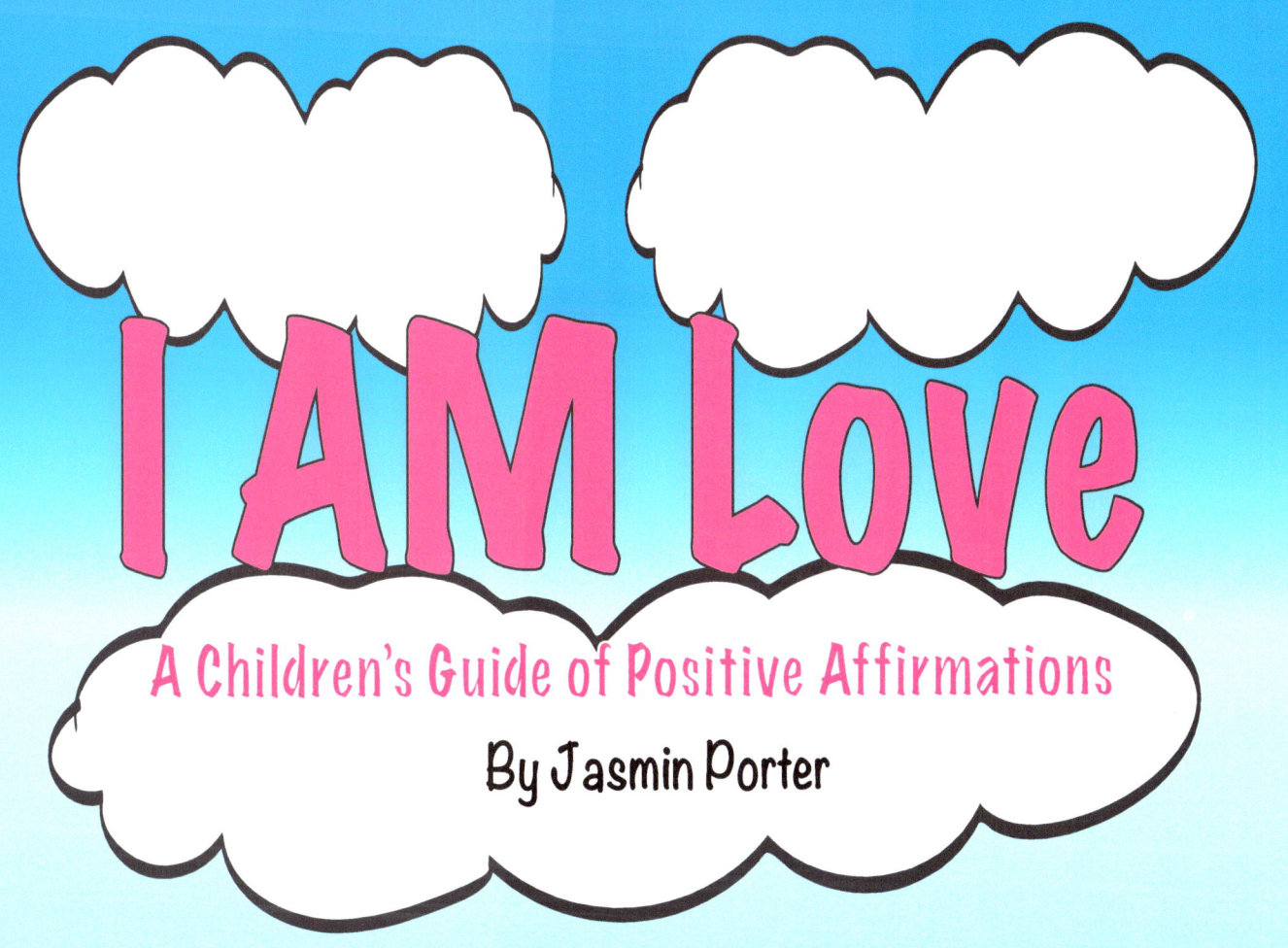

1

I am funny with a smile that is so lovely!

3

I am beautiful
with hair that is tight and coily!

5

I am the sun, moon, and the stars!

I am all of those things because my light shines very far!

9

I am smart and I am fantastic!

11

I am what you call magnificent!

I am special from the top of my head all the way down to the tip of my toes!

15

I am beautiful, yes I say.
Even my round
pudgy nose!

17

I am my weight, my height, my skin, and my hair!

Yes, I am all of those things because they make up who I am!

21

I am Mother Nature because she is so still and peaceful!

23

I am a tree, yes a tree, because their importance is meaningful!

I am important because
I am loved!

27

I am unique because I come from the stars above!

By the way, thank you tree for supplying the oxygen that we all need to breathe!

31

I am healthy just like the healthy foods that I eat!

33

I am comforting just like tight hugs!

35

What is my name you asked?

37

Well, that is simple!

39

I am love you see, I am radiating in Positive Energy!

www.ingramcontent.com/pod-product-compliance
Lightning Source LLC
Chambersburg PA
CBHW041154290426
44108CB00002B/63